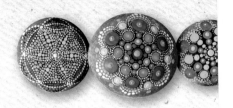

Paint Your Own

MaNDaLa
STONeS

h
hinkler

KaTie CaMeRON

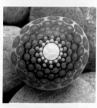

Mandala Stones

The word 'mandala' comes from Sanskrit and means 'circle'. Traditional mandalas show a square enclosed within a circle. They are mystical symbols of the universe, representing life itself. Native Americans, Tibetans and people from many other cultures created mandalas. Hindus and Buddhists use them as meditation aids. Today the word mandala can refer to any geometric pattern inspired by these ancient symbols.

Creating beautiful mandala art on stones is a wonderful way to spend a few hours. You don't need to be a skilled painter to create these colourful artworks – anyone can do it! The act of painting mandalas can be relaxing and therapeutic, very much like meditation.

Mandalas involve symmetry and geometry. They can be as simple as a few circles or more complex in design. Mandalas on stones are tangible and lasting, and allow you to experience and appreciate their beauty and magnetism.

There are eight activities in this book, progressing from simple to intricate pieces. The simple designs allow you to develop skills before completing the more intricate activities. The intricate designs are not necessarily difficult to create, but they do take more time. Patience and a steady hand are key to creating these lovely mandala stones.

CONTENTS

Getting started 3

Radiating-Dot Mandala 8

Petal Pattern 10

Colour-Drop Mandala 12

Stained-Glass Flower 14

Seed of Life 16

Gem Mandala 18

Kaleidoscope Mandala 20

Nature-Inspired Mandala 22

Congratulations and a Note on the Author 24

GETTING STARTED

YOU WILL NEED A FEW THINGS BEFORE YOU CAN GET STARTED ON YOUR ACTIVITIES.

STONES

The best stones to create mandalas on are smooth and relatively free of cracks or holes. Stones that are too rough or pitted are not ideal because the paint will run and neat detailing is difficult to achieve. Rounded stones make for nice symmetry, although you can create mandalas on stones of any shape. Keep in mind that generally the larger the stone, the longer it will take to complete.

If you are going to gather your own stones (rock hunting is often half the fun!), smooth stones are most often found along the shores of oceans and rivers. But if this is not an option or you want to save time, smooth stones can be purchased from craft stores.

> **IMPORTANT:** *Make sure it is OK to take the stones from your area. Some places have regulations to protect the environment against things like erosion or risks to animal habitats, and sometimes it can also be culturally inappropriate. Ensure that you always ask permission if taking from private property.*

Be sure to thoroughly clean your stones. Rinse off the bulk of any mud or sand outside (not down the kitchen drain!), and then give it a scrub in the sink with soap and water. You want to ensure that the stones you are going to paint are free of any dust or debris and are completely dry before you begin.

WORK SPACE

You will need a large, well-lit work space with enough space for you to paint and also have everything you need within arm's reach. Your station should be high enough to maintain good posture, and be equipped with a comfortable chair. Painting these beautiful stones can take a lot of time, but be aware of the time you're spending and try not to sit for too long! Be sure to get up, stretch and move around for ten minutes or so at least once an hour. Movement is good for your body's circulation and can also help you refocus.

To keep your work space neat and tidy, place a piece of cardboard or paper towel beneath your stone before you begin, and protect the remainder of your space with old newspaper. The cardboard helps to keep the underside of the stone clean and can also be helpful if you wish to move the stone to another area without needing to pick it up.

HANDY HINT

Have the paint colours you plan to use, or have been using, set aside. This comes in handy if you are mixing a new shade, picking up where you left off, or if you are applying a second coat. You don't want to apply a second coat in the wrong colour!

PAINTS

There is no need to purchase expensive paints to create your mandala stones – cheap acrylic craft paint generally works well. Acrylic paint is non-toxic, easy to clean up (just use soap and water), and is relatively fast to dry.

When it comes to choosing colours and shades of paint, start with the basic primary colours. You can always mix new colour combinations or adjust shades with a little bit of white or black. Most acrylic paint of the same brand is easily intermixable. Use a small container to mix in, making sure that it has a lid – this way you won't waste paint and you will have the exact shade to use another time. I use old, small craft paint pots and empty lip gloss containers.

Varying the colours (dark versus light) for the base coat of your stone will create a different visual effect by way of contrast.

For texture, try adding a dot a shade lighter on top of your finished dots, i.e. a slightly paler purple on a dark purple coloured dot. The size and arrangement of shades of dots can also create a 3D effect.

Drying time for acrylic paint can be anywhere from 15–30 minutes, depending on the thickness of the paint; though this is 'to the touch'. It can take 24 hours or more for acrylic craft paint to 'cure' to a point where it is completely dry and at maximum hardness, and this can be affected by many factors like temperature, humidity, type of paint, brand and colour. Do not touch the stone while it is drying or you risk leaving smudges or fingerprints. Even after you have allowed the paint to dry, applying the clear finish can moisten it again for a short time. The last thing you want at this final stage is a paint mishap, so hands off until you're sure the paint is firm!

NOTES ON MIXING COLOURS

When I started out doing mandala stones, I had only the basic primary colours (red, yellow and blue) and secondary colours (green, orange and purple). I would use a small plate to mix up small dabs of colour using trial and error. I've learned that you can create tertiary colours by mixing one primary and one secondary colour to get yellow-orange, orange-red, red-violet, violet-blue, blue-green, or yellow-green.

HANDY HINT

If you find you absolutely love painting mandalas (and you will!), you'll probably want to purchase more colours of paint. Many craft stores have 'value packs' with a few shades of every colour at a cheaper price than it costs to buy each colour individually. For even more savings, wait until the store has a sale and purchase that value pack!

Lightening your acrylic paint colours with white paint is called 'tinting'. Each colour has a limit on how much lighter it can become, called its 'tinting strength'. Dark colours have a higher tinting strength because they start off darker, giving them more space to be made lighter. To lighten, just add a small amount of white paint to the colour.

Adding black paint to a lighter acrylic paint colour makes it turn darker. This is called 'shading'. Keep in mind that black is strong, so a little paint goes a long way.

TOOLS

There are a few tools that are useful to have when creating mandala stones:

- Pencil and eraser – use these to sketch out your ideas and designs on paper beforehand. Light markings in a grey-lead pencil can be used directly on the stone or dry paint, and an eraser can be used to remove any marks or you can simply paint over them.

- Drawing compass and ruler – you can use your eye to judge measurements like centre points for designs and base coats, but a ruler and compass make this process much faster and easier. Where symmetry is an important factor in creating mandalas, you will want precise and equal measurements on all sides. These tools will also help to guide your creative process when forming new designs on paper. A compass may be difficult to use on some shapes of stones; if this is the case just use your judgement to visually choose the centre spot.

- Paintbrushes – pointed brushes are best for fine detailing and lines, dotting and touch-ups. Use a larger sized round or flat brush when painting areas that need a more coverage, i.e. base coats. Generally brushes with shorter handles and shorter, firmer bristles are better to achieve precise detailing. Dot formation will vary with the amount of paint on the brush and how much pressure you use. For larger dots, use brush with larger bristles. It is important to keep your brushes in good condition with the bristles straight and together. Never allow brushes to dry with paint on them, and only dip them into the paint to about half the hair length. This is so you do not allow paint to get on the ferrule (the little metal piece that attaches the bristles to brush handle). Getting the ferrule in the paint will inevitably result in spreading and frayed bristles, no matter how much you wash your

HANDY HINT

If you have a lot of paints and store them in a drawer or container where you cannot see each label, brush a dab of paint on the top of the lid. This way you can easily see which colour is which, and how it will look when dry. When you only have a few small dots to do, you can save paint by dipping your stick in the paint that is left behind on the cap after you shake the container, rather than pouring it onto a palette. Just don't forget to put the cap back on!

paintbrush. I recommend having a little cup of water at your work station so that you can quickly wash off paint and keep brushes moist before washing them thoroughly with soap and water.

- Dotting tools – you can use specialist dotting tools to do dot work, or you can save money by using the pointed ends of household items. Think toothpicks, skewers, small dowels, unsharpened pencil ends, etc. These items allow you to have greater precision and control when doing intricate dot work, and care is minimal as you do not have to clean them! You can allow the paint to dry on the sticks, which can layer and create new sizes for their ends; or you can pull off the dried paint and have a small, pointed end once more.

HaNDY HINT

If you're using dowels as dotting tools, you can sharpen them with a pencil sharpener or blade to create a variety of dotting sizes.

MaKING DOTS

I find the easiest way to ensure accuracy when placing dots is to hold the stick in one hand as you would a pencil and, if needed, steady the rock with your other hand. Try to hold the stick vertically to the stone, coming in at a 90-degree angle when applying dots. Steady your aim by resting your hand, wrist or elbow against the desk or the stone itself.

To increase the size of each dot from one row to the next is mostly a matter of having the right amount of paint on the right-sized stick. This is a skill you will need when creating designs such as the Radiating-Dot Mandala. Usually the smaller the point the smaller the dot will be. I use the small pointed end of a toothpick. Another way to achieve very small dots is to use the very tip of the longest bristle in a round paintbrush.

The smallest dots do not require a lot of paint to be on the point to make a well-formed circle-shaped dot. Too much paint and you could accidentally place a dot too large. Generally, if you do not re-dip and use the same amount of pressure with each dot, the size of the next dot will be smaller than the one before it, so you will need to wipe clean and re-dip the stick into the paint after each dot to maintain saturation and equal dot sizing.

When you want to go up in the size of a dot, you can use the same size dotting tool saturated in slightly more paint and add just a bit more pressure while touching the stick to stone. If you do not wipe

the paint from the stick before re-dipping, it will start to dry and accumulate, enlarging the end of the tool. A bigger tool end will give a bigger size dot.

To increase dot size you can also use a larger tool. The diameter of the end of the tool you are using is a good indication of the size of the dot it will create and of course the more it is saturated with paint, the bigger the dot will be.

CLeaR FINISH

Most craft stores stock affordable clear, gloss or matte acrylic finishes that will make your colours appear brighter and seal them in place longer. It will also protect against fading, and make your stones resistant to water and weather conditions. I recommend the spray-on type (as opposed to the brush-on), as this is quick, easy and adheres to all parts of the stone in a uniform, even manner.

Always wait until your stone is complete (not in need of any touch-ups), the paint is completely dry and hard, and the stone is free of any dust or unwanted particles before spraying the protective finish in a well-ventilated room or outside. Allow your stone to sit at least a day for the finish to dry, then apply the second coat and allow to dry again. As with paint, avoid touching your stone while the finish is drying to ensure the coating hardens smoothly.

If you do not wish to use a protective finish, you can try using acrylic 'outdoor' paints which are designed with a finish built in. These outdoor craft paints are indeed more durable than the regular acrylic paints; however, they cost more as well, and are not as durable as using a separate finishing coat.

FIXING MISTAKES, AND OTHER TIPS AND TRICKS

Here are a few other little tips that I'd like to share before you start your mandala-stone journey.

PATIENCE

Mandala stones can take many hours, if not days, to complete. Patience is key during this time. If you try to rush you will likely have to spend even more time fixing a careless mistake that could have easily been avoided. That being said, don't worry too much about tiny imperfections. Often in the grand scheme of things they go unnoticed with all the other details around them.

DOT PRACTICE

Practise, practise, practise! Having precision with dots takes a steady hand and knowing where to place the brush/stick with just the right amount of pressure. Dip your tool into your paint often so that you leave a thick, nicely saturated dot. This helps avoid the need to apply a second coat to your dot, and also minimises the risk of making a mistake. It may also help to do a test dot with the dotting tool and paint on a scrap of paper so you get a feel for how the paint will transfer and the pressure needed to apply an evenly shaped, circular dot, before beginning the activities.

DOT RINGS

Turn the rock as you make dot rings so that you have a good viewpoint and are not reaching over the stone. You want the dots to align with each other as they extend out from the centre, so it is important to turn the stone and get good centred placement in the spaces of the ring before.

DOT FIX

Dropped an uneven dot or made one so big it ran into the others? Depending on where and when in the process this happens, you may be able to wipe the paint away using a bit of water and a brush, or scrape the mistake off with a stick or a bit of fine sandpaper. It is much safer to allow the area (if not the entire stone) to dry before you attempt to fix mistakes. Make sure to clear away any flakes before simply painting the area with the same colour as the underlying coat. Allow this to dry, and reapply your dot. It's like it never happened!

ACRYLIC 'ERASER'

The good thing about acrylic paint is that it is thick enough to paint over and not show through underneath. The base colour is your friend! Use it as an 'eraser' for small mistakes. Don't like a dot colour you have used? Dot right over top of it. Voila!

WONKY MANDALA

If you find you didn't quite start in the middle of your stone and your mandala is off centre to your base circle, use more base paint to even out the circle and centre your mandala. If worse comes to worst and you have messed up more than you think is worth taking the time to fix, scrub off the paint using soap and water. It is just a rock after all.

Before you begin

Plan ahead – sketch out your design idea before you start. Trace the shape of your stone onto a piece of paper so you can get an idea what will fit on your 'canvas'. Use your ruler and drawing compass to practise making circles and other geometric shapes. It is helpful to get the hang of a pattern on paper before it's set on stone.

Practise making dots! It might seem an easy enough task but you will soon find out they can be rather tricky. Find your favourite tool to use and practise on paper or another rock. If you are using sticks you will find you need to dip them at least every second dot to maintain even dot size and saturation. If you are still having trouble, try a different vantage on the stone by turning it often, picking it up, or adjusting the angle at which you touch the paint to the stone.

Always keep in mind there is no right or wrong way to make your mandala stone; not everyone uses the same method or follows the steps in the same order. These are simply some suggestions on one way to go about it. Everyone has a different technique so it is important to find what works best for you!

Keep calm and dot on!

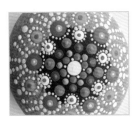 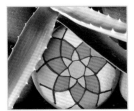 

radiating-dot mandala

THIS IS a SIMPLE STARTER MANDALA YOU CAN PAINT THAT WILL ALLOW YOU TO PRACTISE MAKING DOTS. IT MAY BE SIMPLE IN DESIGN BUT ITS VIBRANT RAINBOW OF COLOURS REALLY MAKES IT STAND OUT AND GET NOTICED. AS YOU WILL SEE, YOU CAN PAINT THIS STYLE ON ANY SHAPE OF STONE AND ALWAYS HAVE PLEASING RESULTS.

YOU WILL NEED:

Stone

Compass and pencil

Paintbrushes: large, small

Dotting tools: small, medium, large

Paint: black, red, purple, dark blue, blue, green, yellow, orange

Protective finish

1 Determine which side of your stone you want to paint. It is best to have the stone lying flat so it does not wobble while you are painting. Try laying it on either side to see which is more stable and, surface permitting, paint whichever side is up when the stone lies flat.

2 Find the centre point of the side you will paint. This does not have to be an exact measurement. If your stone is an irregular shape, one way to accurately estimate this point is to use the compass to make the largest full circle that will fit on the stone's shape. You do not have to draw this circle (if you do, just erase the markings after), but do mark where the pointed end of the compass stands with a pencil, as this is your centre point.

3 Place your compass at the centre point, but set its angle so you can draw a circle that covers about three-quarters of the surface of the stone. Paint the base coat – this is the underlying colour for your mandala design. Rather than cover the entire stone in paint (though that is certainly an option), paint the main area that will sit under your mandala. Using a larger brush, paint the circle with black paint. Allow to dry for 15–20 minutes or until dry to the touch. Apply a second coat if needed (if the colour of the rock shows through) and allow to dry to the touch.

4 Begin your radiating-dot mandala design with a single centre icon. Using a medium dotting tool or dowel, dip the end in red paint, saturating it well, and carefully place the first dot on the centre point. The dotting tool should be saturated enough so the paint easily transfers to the stone without the dotting tool really needing to touch the stone itself. You may need to lightly apply pressure and tilt the dotting tool around in a circular motion to even the edges until the red paint has formed a circular dot. You can continue to the next steps without needing to wait for the dot to dry between steps.

5 Take one of your smallest dotting tools (I used the end of a toothpick), and place about 12 very small, evenly spaced purple dots in a ring around the red centre icon. Distance these small dots out from the icon equally while leaving room for them to sit without touching each other or the centre icon. If you find you have trouble evenly spacing your dots, it can help to mark these spots with a pencil and paint over.

6 Moving out from the centre, paint another ring of purple dots that are slightly larger than the first, turning the stone as you dot. You can use the same small stick and same colour paint. Dip the small dotting tool in the paint before each dot. You may need to wipe it off every so often to maintain its size, because the paint will start to accumulate on it after a short time. Place the dots in line with the small spaces left between the first ring of dots. Spacing them evenly should be easy now, as you have the small dots as reference.

7 Continue adding dots in this manner, working your way out from the centre icon towards the edges of the stone. The next two rings of dots after purple will be dark blue, followed by two each of blue, green, yellow, orange and finishing with red. As you begin each new ring, increase the size of the dots slightly, while maintaining even spacing between each dot and their proximity to the dots in the ring before them.

As you increase dot size for the next row of the same colour, rather than wiping the dotting tool, allow the paint to accumulate. This creates a greater surface area for the paint on the stick and will make a larger size of dot for the following row; though you must wipe the dowel clean or use a different one when changing colours. You can also increase the size of the dotting tool as needed.

8 When you have completed dotting the stone with two rings of dots in each colour, allow your stone to dry for at least 20–30 minutes.

9 Touch-up time! Once the dots have dried, apply a second coat of the same colour to any dots that look like they could use it. Paint looks full and vibrant while wet, but when dry you can often see where you may not

have applied enough paint. This is when you should also touch up any minor mistakes you may have made along the way. Use the tip of your smallest brush to get into tight places that require steady accuracy. Allow any touch-ups to dry for 20–30 minutes.

10 Allow your finished stone to dry completely, for at least a few hours to ensure the paint has hardened. Leaving it overnight would be best.

11 Once your dot work has dried, apply a coat of clear protective finish. Allow to dry at least a few hours, then repeat with a second coat of finish. Wait 24 hours to ensure the paint and finish coats have dried and hardened completely.

HaNDY HINT

The number of dots in each circle of colour is not important so long as they are small and all of relatively equal size and spacing. The rainbow colour spectrum is ordered R.O.Y.G.B.I.V... that is red, orange, yellow, green, blue, indigo (dark blue), violet (purple). These dots move out from the centre going in the reverse order: V.I.B.G.Y.O.R.

PETAL PATTERN

THIS SIMPLE FLORAL DESIGN USES DOTS, LINES AND TRIANGULAR SHAPES ORGANISED ON A SQUARE GRID. THE COLOUR REALLY STANDS OUT AGAINST THE WHITE BACKGROUND, AND THE FINISHED PIECE HAS A GREAT FEEL AND TEXTURE. TRY SKETCHING OUT THE PATTERN DISCUSSED ON PAPER BEFORE YOU BEGIN SO THAT YOU CAN PRACTISE AND GET AN IDEA OF WHAT WILL FIT ON YOUR STONE.

YOU WILL NEED:

- Stone
- Ruler and pencil
- Paintbrush: small
- Dotting tools: small, medium
- Paint: white, pink
- Protective finish

HANDY HINT

The number of dots in each circle of colour is not important so long as they are small and all of relatively equal size and spacing.

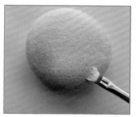

1 Begin by painting the stone all over with the base colour (white) and allow to dry to the touch. You will only paint a single coat at this time.

2 Using a ruler and pencil, very lightly make a square grid centred on the stone. You'll need to paint over this later (or gently use an eraser if it doesn't affect the paint on the base coat) so make sure it is as fine as possible. Start by finding the approximate centre point and draw a line horizontally and vertically that intersects this point. Measure and form the grid so that it has one large square with four smaller squares within it that intersect with the centre point.

3 Grab a medium-sized dotting tool and pink paint, and carefully place the larger centre icon dot on the point where the grid intersects in the centre of the stone. Set aside the medium-sized dotting tool and use the smallest size tool to continue painting 8–12 small dots around the centre icon. Ensure that one dot is on each of the four gridlines as you circle the centre icon.

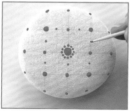

4 Continue with the small dotting tool and pink paint. Go around the stone and place a medium dot at each of the 4 corners of the large square (this is approximately the four corners of the stone as well). These are the centre points of each small 'corner' flower. Continue placing small pink dots at every other intersection that does not yet have one. These are the centres to the 'line' petals seen at 12, 3, 6 and 9 o'clock on the grid.) Finally place a dot on the midpoint of each side of each of the 4 small squares in the grid. You will already have dots at the intersections to these squares. These dots are reference points for when you form petals in the next step.

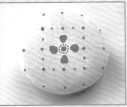

5 Return to the centre. Using a small paintbrush, form the four large triangular-shaped petals along the gridlines of the centre icon, and then four around each of the four corner dots.

HaNDY HINT

To add extra feel-appeal, you can add dots in white paint in some of the empty space on your stone if you wish. I have done this on my stone.

6 Paint in the thin 'line' petals pointing towards the four corners (of your larger square) between each of the four larger petals. Repeat for each of the four corner points of the stone – the top left, right, bottom left and right corners. Form the diamond pattern of dot detailing. Place four dots in a line diagonally that extend out from the centre petals to meet the midpoint reference of each of the sides of the perimeter. Then do another four dots to the tip of the diamond, and eight on the way back, mirroring the opposite side. Do this at 12, 3, 6 and 9 o'clock positions.

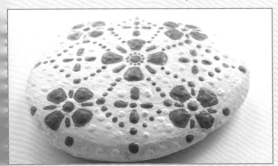

7 Using your small dotting tool, dot a line extending out from each point of the diamond over the edge of the stone. Using a thin paintbrush, dot in each of the four line petals within each diamond. Allow to dry completely and apply another coat of colour if needed. Allow that to dry too, and then use a

fine white paintbrush to paint over your gridlines, or an eraser if you have one. (Test it on the back of the stone before using on the front!) Because of the many layers of paint I recommend leaving your stone a full day to dry before coating in protective finish.

8 Protect your art using two coats of protective finish, allowing to dry between coats.

COLOUR-DROP MANDALA

THESE LITTLE GEMS DO NOT REQUIRE MUCH PLANNING. THEY COME IN ALL SHAPES AND SIZES AND ARE EASIER TO MAKE THAN THEY LOOK! YOU WILL FIND THEY OFTEN TEND TO MAKE UP THEIR OWN PATTERN AS YOU GO.

YOU WILL NEED:

- Stone
- Ruler, compass and pencil
- Paintbrush: large
- Dotting tools: small, medium, large
- Paint: black, white, purple, light purple, dark red, pink, pale pink, bright pink, yellow, light yellow, orange, bright red
- Protective finish

1 Use your ruler to measure out where the centre point should be on your chosen stone. Then use the compass and pencil to draw a base circle around this point. The circle should cover about half the surface area.

2 Use the large brush to paint the base circle black. Allow to dry 10–15 minutes or to the touch.

3 Begin the mandala with a centre icon. Use a large dotting tool dipped in white paint to carefully place a white dot at the centre point of the base circle. Use a medium dotting tool to paint six evenly spaced, smaller purple dots that circle the centre icon, leaving a small space between each of them. You should dip the dowel in the paint before each dot so that you have the same amount of paint and pressure each time. Use your smallest dotting tool to dot six tiny white dots in between the purple dots surrounding the centre icon.

4 Using the medium-sized dotting tool and a lighter shade of purple, add another ring of slightly larger dots, fitting them snugly in the small spaces between the purple dots you just made, above the tiny white dots. Continue this way, adding another ring of slightly larger, dark red dots in the space between those left by the ring before. The next ring of slightly larger dots is done using a pink colour.

5 Now that you are nearing the edge of the base circle, use the medium-sized dotting tool and white paint to place the next ring of dots out slightly further out from the previous set. Keep these dots about the same size as the pink dots and leave a bit of space – enough so that you can surround these white dots with tiny dots of a contrasting pale pink colour.

HANDY HINT

To get that eye-catching contrast of colour and detailed look, keep the dots as close as possible without allowing the paint to touch. Use a dark colour for the base so the brighter colours stand out more.

6 Using the dotting tool with the smallest point, carefully place a tiny pale pink dot in a ring around each of the white dots. The first dot will be slightly larger than the rest since it is freshly dipped in paint, but don't dip your tool again until you reach half way around the circle. You should now have a tiny gradual tapered ring of pale pink around each white dot.

HANDY HINT

The process of tapering dots is used in some of the different activities in this book. Keep this term in mind as you'll see it again later!

7 Using a large dotting tool and bright red paint, place a dot in the space out from each pink dot. Again, place these red dots so there is enough space to add a ring of tiny yellow dots around each of them. Once the red dots are done, surround each with tiny yellow dots. By now you will have extended out beyond the base coat and onto the rock with your dots. Take extra care here as mistakes can be a lot harder to fix on the bare rock.

8 Switching back to your medium-sized dotting tool, place smaller orange dots in the spaces between the red dots. Size the orange dots so that they can be ringed with tiny white dots.

9 This time when adding the tiny white dots around the orange, instead of creating a circle, stop where you start to meet the tiny pink dots on the inner edge and form an arc of white dots around the orange dots.

10 Continue using a small dotting tool and dot four small light yellow dots directly above the top of the outer edge of the four yellow dots that circle the large red dot. Now use white paint to add dotted lines fan outward and end in a larger dot at the end of the fan, and a dot on the outer edge of each orange dot. This creates a drip-and-splash look like a droplet of water. Allow the paint to dry to the touch.

11 If needed, go over your art again using a small stick. Using the same colours add smaller contrasting colours to the dots: light purple on the dark red, bright pink on the pink, dark red on the white, bright red on the orange, orange on the bright red, then topping that with white.

12 Allow your stone to dry completely for at least a couple hours. Spray with 2 coats of protective finish.

STAINED-GLASS FLOWER

THE STAINED-GLASS LOOK IS ACHIEVED BY DRAWING THE DESIGN MOSTLY FREEHAND AND USING THICK DARK LINES BETWEEN THE VARIOUS COLOURS. YOU WILL WANT TO PRACTISE DRAWING THIS ON PAPER BEFOREHAND.

YOU WILL NEED:

- Stone
- Ruler and pencil
- Paintbrushes: small, large
- Paint: black, purple, magenta, light green, light yellow, light brown, light blue, light purple, light pink, blue, peach
- Protective finish

1   Using a pencil, draw the outline of the design on the rock. Begin in the centre and draw or trace a heptagon (seven-sided polygon shape). Using a ruler or straight edge, draw lines out from the middle point of each side and each corner of the heptagon. These lines will indicate the point where the tip of your triangle or 'petal' crosses over to form the beginning of the next petal.

2   Starting at one of the flat sides of the heptagon, from the corner, draw slightly curved lines inwards and upwards to meet and intersect with each other at the point in the line you have drawn, thus forming the first small triangle. Continue doing this all the way around at each side and moving away from the centre.

3   At the outer tip of the triangle, draw a line outwards to form a point, and do the same from the next triangle tip around. Essentially the line from the left side of one small triangle and the right side of the one next to it form a new larger petal between each of the small triangle petals. Then, continue these new lines out to the edge of the stone.

4   Using a small brush and black paint, go over these lines that outline the petals. Allow to dry 15–20 minutes or to the touch. Do not worry too much if your lines aren't straight or of an even width; you can adjust them using the coloured paint in the next step.

5   Using a larger brush and purple paint, paint the centre shape and the 7 small triangles. If you need to, paint over the black outline to even it up or straighten it out. Paint the next petals magenta, and those after that with light green, light yellow, light brown, light blue, light purple, light pink and blue.

6 Use a peach colour to paint beyond your final petals. Allow to dry, then paint a second coat. Allow this to dry again for 20 minutes or to the touch.

7 Carefully go over your outline again using a small brush and black paint. Again, even out any colouring if necessary.

8 When you are satisfied with your creation and it has dried completely, spray it evenly with at least two coats of protective finish. Allow to dry overnight between coats.

SEED OF LIFE

THIS DESIGN IS TAKEN FROM THE MIDDLE OF A 'SEED OF LIFE' GEOMETRIC PATTERN AND IS INTRICATELY LAID OUT ON THE STONE IN DOTS! YOU CAN MAKE JUST ONE OR IF YOU ARE USING A LARGE ROCK YOU CAN CONTINUE MAKING THE PATTERN ACROSS THE ENTIRE STONE.

YOU WILL NEED:

- Stone
- Compass and pencil
- Paintbrush: large
- Dotting tools: small, medium
- Paint: black, white, aqua, light blue, turqoise, purple, green
- Protective finish

1 Use a large brush to paint a large black base circle and allow to dry. Using your compass, sketch the middle of the 'seed of life' design onto the stone. Start at the centre and use the compass to make a circle around the edge (on top of the black base paint). Leaving the angle of the compass the same, move the centre point of the compass to a starting point anywhere on the outer edge of your base circle. From this point, create a half-circle arc across the stone.

2 Move the compass to the point where the half circle you just made meets the opposite edge of the circle, and make another half-circle arc across the stone. Continue moving your compass and making half circles in this way until your flower outline is complete! (Six half circles in total.)

3 Use a pencil to draw in the curved lines that connect each tip of the 'petals'. It is easier to do this freehand.

4 Start painting in the middle where all petals intersect. With a medium-sized dotting tool and white paint, place a centre dot icon. Switch to a smaller dotting tool and surround the centre icon with six smaller white dots on each petal line. Place a white dot at each point where the petals meet the outer circle and, using slightly smaller dots, go over the remainder of the outline you have made with tight, evenly spaced white dots.

5 Moving beyond the base circle, place a white dot on the side of the rock at equal intervals between those larger dots that make up the petal tips. Then connect the petal tips to this outer dot, forming a triangle shape that curves over the side.

6 Using a small dotting tool, colour in the petals with tapered paint dots. Remember to space them and try not to touch dots together. Begin at the midpoint on the inner edge of each petal with a dot of aqua coloured paint, dot middle to tip, then middle to centre icon, creating gradually smaller dots in each direction. This should leave you with a small inner-petal space that you can fill with a light blue line of tapered dots. Then, use turquoise paint to dot the space between petals.

7 Continue with purple for the spaces between petal tips within the base circle, and green for the spaces you made on the edge of the stone in step 5.

8 Allow the dots to try completely and spray with two coats of protective finish. Allow to dry overnight between coats.

GEM MANDALA

THIS MANDALA STONE ALWAYS GETS NOTICED! THE JEWEL IN THE CENTRE IS OPTIONAL, BUT ADDS TO THE COLOURFUL ARRAY OF DOTS THAT MAKE UP THIS EYE-CATCHING TREASURE.

YOU WILL NEED:

- Stone
- Compass and pencil
- Paintbrushes: small, large
- Dotting tools: small, medium, large
- Paint: black, white, purple, magenta, dark mauve, light pink, red, orange, light orange, green, turquoise, light green, yellow, blue, aqua, light blue
- Protective finish
- Optional: gem

1 Select a smooth stone and, using a compass at the centre point, form a base circle on the stone encompassing about two-thirds of the stone's centre. Paint the circle using a large brush and black paint.

2 Using a large dotting tool, carefully place a white dot at the centre point. Make this icon big enough to fit a jewel if you plan to use one, but don't stick it on yet! Use a medium-sized dotting tool and purple paint to surround the centre icon with eight evenly spaced dots, leaving space between them to allow for one very small magenta dot. These dots should be as close to the centre icon as possible without touching.

3 Continuing with your medium-sized dotting tool, dip into the magenta paint and place the next ring of slightly larger dots in the spaces that are above that small magenta dot, between the purple dots.

4 The next dot in this pattern sequence is painted in the colour dark mauve. Use a medium-sized dotting tool to place these dots out from the previous dots, leaving space to encircle them all with tiny, light pink dots; then do the tiny dots. Add very tiny white dots around the large centre circle, either side of each magenta dot.

5 Between these dark mauve and light pink circled dots, place a red dot (smaller than the magenta dot before it). Next, using a medium dotting-tool, place a larger orange dot directly above these red dots. Again, leave room so that you may encircle each of the orange dots with a tiny, light orange tapered circle of dots. Rather than ring all the way around the orange dot, stop the tiny light orange dots on either side of the small red dot when you reach it.

6 Using the medium-sized dotting tool, place eight large dots of green paint in the spaces between the orange ringed dots. By now you should have reached the edge of the black base circle, and just be starting to paint bare rock.

7 Using a large dotting tool or a small brush and turquoise paint, add in large dots the same size as the centre icon on the outer edge of the green dots. Allow enough space on the outer edge so that you can add in at least three rings of small dots encircling each.

8 With a tiny dotting tool and light green paint, carefully place a tight ring around each of these large turquoise dots. Follow this ring with another ring of small, tapered yellow dots. This yellow ring ends on either side of the green dot (directly in from the turquoise dot). Use white paint to form the final dotted ring around the turquoise dot.

9 In the small amount of space left over between these white rings and the orange-ringed dot, use a small dotting tool to create a dotted line of 'drip' down the sides of the rock. Use the colours blue, purple, red, orange and yellow, slightly decreasing in size as you move down the edges of the stone. Allow to dry to the touch for 30 minutes or more.

10 Once all your dots have dried, add in dots on top of the dots! Start with the dark mauve ones and place a magenta dot (the same magenta colour as the dots before it) in the centre on top of the dark mauve dots. Make sure the underlying colour can still be seen by only covering the underlying dot by 50% at most. On top of the orange and green dots place a smaller yellow dot. Finally on top of the large turquoise dots place a medium aqua dot. Allow this dot to dry to the touch and add an even smaller dot of light blue on top of the aqua dots.

11 Allow the paint to set overnight, then apply two coats of the protective finish, allowing to dry between coats.

This one is optional! After applying varnish and allowing the final coat to dry, you can stick a jewel to the centre of this mandala stone. You can find these at craft stores. If you do not have adhesive-backed ones, take a file or other abrasive device and lightly scratch away some of the varnish off the centre dot. This is to help the jewel adhere to the stone.

KALEIDOSCOPE MANDALA

I created this design as a birthday gift for my mother. I wanted to paint something original, with details like hearts and flowers – because what mother doesn't love hearts and flowers? I found some detail inspiration in Dutch folk-art designs, and used my imagination and favourite colours for the end result. Now you can make one for someone special, too!

YOU WILL NEED:

- Stone
- Compass, pencil and paper
- Paintbrushes: small, large
- Dotting tools: small, medium
- Paint: light grey, dark green, navy blue, bright yellow, peach, orange, light yellow, dark yellow, green, turquoise, light green, white, red, yellow, purple, light purple, pink, light blue
- Protective finish

1 Use a large brush to paint the stone all over, top and sides, in light grey paint. Allow to dry to the touch. Use your compass to draw a large circle around the edge of your stone. Paint this circle on top of the first layer using dark green paint. Allow to dry 20 minutes or to the touch. Make a smaller circle with the compass, inside the green circle, and paint this navy blue. Allow all paint to dry to the touch. You now have three base colours top to bottom: navy, dark green, light grey.

2 Start the mandala with a dot icon in the centre of the stone. Use a medium-sized dotting tool to carefully place a bright yellow dot at the centre point. Surround this icon by six smaller peach dots. Space these peach dots slightly out from the centre icon and leave space between them to place six tiny orange dots.

3 Using the small dotting tool, do the tiny orange dots. Then place a small dot of light yellow directly above each orange dot. Fit in a small dark yellow dot on either side of these light yellow ones, just above the peach dots.

HANDY HINT

When placing dots, it helps to look at both the micro and macro view. Macro: to get an idea of the stone as a whole and what image the arrangement of dots is creating. Micro: reviewing how each dot is placed in reference to those dots around it. Each dot has other dots that it align with it in some way.

4 Using a medium-sized dotting tool and green paint, place a small dot directly above each light yellow dot, as well as another larger green dot directly above the space between the dark yellow dots (above the peach dots). This dot work should now be forming a hexagon shape.

5 Use a small brush and turquoise paint to create the teardrop shapes. The large end should sit above each of the smaller green dots that make up the middle of each side of the 'hexagon'. Make the teardrop tip end at the arc of the navy base circle without going into the dark green base. Use a small dotting tool and light green paint to dot very small dots, close together, all around the line where the navy base circle meets the dark green. Repeat this using small orange dots just above the ring of light green ones.

6 To get the cut-out look at the side of the stone, place the corner of a piece of paper in line with each teardrop tip so you know where to start and stop the dots. With a piece of paper in place, leave a gap after the last ring of dots and circle the stone again with white paint, slightly in from the edge of the green base circle (enough for another circle of dots).

7 Finally, circle the edge of the dark green base circle using red dots outside the white. Use a small brush to paint over the green triangles (which were under the paper) using the grey base paint. Allow to dry for at least 30 minutes.

8 While you allow the sides to dry you can add tiny dot detailing along the outside edges of the teardrops. Using your smallest dotting tool and yellow paint, outline in a fine dotted line all along the outside of the teardrop, stopping at the dot at each end of the petal.

9 Place tiny white dots next to the tiny yellow dots that outline around the teardrops, adding a bright yellow teardrop at the end of each turquoise teardrop.

10 Place two red dots, one above the other, in the space between each turquise teardrop. It will lie just above the large green dot in the corners of the hexagon. Place a few purple dots splitting in either direction along these white dots.

11 Use the dark green base paint and small brush to paint over the navy blue in the space between these purple dots.

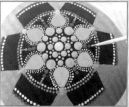

12 Allow to dry and place three tiny turquoise dots above where the red ones split off, extending to the first ring of light green.

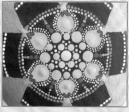

13 Add in dot detailing on top of other dots and petals. Create the red hearts on the tip of the turquoise teardrops by slightly dragging the paint away from the dot once placed. You could also use your smallest paintbrush.

14 Place a light green dot on the rounded part of the teardrop and allow it to dry, then place a smaller light purple dot on top of it; finally add pink on the light purple. Outline the inner teardrops with tiny pink dots atop the turquoise. Add a ring of light blue dots inside the pink and a dot on top of each yellow teardrop. Add light yellow in the centre of the green dots and centre dot.

15 Allow the paint to set overnight, then apply two coats of the protective finish, allowing to dry between coats.

NATURE-INSPIRED MANDALA

THIS DESIGN WAS INSPIRED BY A TRIP TO MY LOCAL NATURAL HISTORY MUSEUM, WHICH FEATURES INTERESTING DISPLAYS OF TRADITIONAL CLOTHING MADE BY THE MI'KMAQ FIRST NATION PEOPLE. THEIR CLOTHING USED INTRICATE BEAD-WORK AND WAS DYED USING EARTH COLOURS SUCH AS RED AND YELLOW OCHRE, WHITE FROM SHELLS, AND BLACK FROM CHARCOAL.

YOU WILL NEED:

- Stone
- Compass and pencil
- Paintbrushes: small, large
- Dotting tools: small, large,
- Paint: dark red, black, mustard, white, orange, bright yellow, light plum, off-white, dark yellow, dark plum, dark orange, yellow, red, purple, navy blue, turquoise, light blue
- Protective finish

1 Paint the stone all over using a large paintbrush and dark red paint. Once this layer has dried, use your compass to draw the next circle, covering about half the rock, and paint it black. Allow to dry, then draw a circle in the centre of the black space and paint it mustard yellow.

4 Use a small dotting tool and yellow paint to dot along the line where the black base circle ends. Use microdots of orange below the yellow (into the black) and small dots of red above it (into the dark red). Place slightly larger dots of mustard yellow above this ring. Allow the stone to dry to touch.

2 Starting in the centre of the yellow circle, place a small white dot icon. Surround it with eight equally spaced smaller dots of white. Place a dot of orange between each white dot. Using a bright yellow colour, add dots that are slightly off the base yellow and dot above the orange, leaving space between each for a light plum dot.

HANDY HINT

The micro dots that you see at the corners of these orange and yellow dots are accomplished using a small brush and allowing the tip of the brush to saturate one tiny bead of paint which you carefully place on the stone. Practise on paper to see what the micro dot will look like before trying on the stone.

3 Place a mirco dot of off-white either side of the light plum dots. Dot one black dot above each bright yellow dot. At the arc edge between base colours, place dots of dark yellow exactly on the line, bridging into the next base colour. Continue circling around the stone with tightly packed dots, graduating the colour shades for each row starting with dark plum, then dark red and smaller dots of dark orange in the spaces between the dark red. Follow these by tiny dots of dark yellow and finish with micro dots of off-white.

5 Place eight purple dots of equal size and spacing directly over top of those rings of yellow you painted in step 4, keeping these in line with the light plum dots you made back in the centre mustard base. Directly above this purple dot and on top of the mustard yellow ring dots, place a larger dot of navy blue. These navy blue dots are then encircled by tiny white dots, and circled again with a half circle of off-white dots.

6 In the spaces between the navy dots along the edge of the stone, use a large dotting tool to place a large turquoise dot. Encircle each turquoise dot with tiny dots of light blue, then purple, mustard yellow, and finally tapered dots of white.

7 Add in the designs in the middle of the stone on the black base. Start by lining up a small orange dot with the black dots in the centre circle as well as the purple and navy dots of the outer rings. With white paint, use a thin brush to make three tiny fanned-out lines from this orange dot. Top each of these lines with a small off-white dot.

8 Use a small dotting tool to add in the arched dots of light plum that go between the inner and outer circles. Start at the midpoint between each orange dot and dot upward and outward, meeting at the purple dot of the next baseline. Then do the same back in.

9 Allow the stone to dry to the touch and go over it once again, making any touch-ups, painting any second coats if needed and adding in any fine detailing you may have missed. Add the light blue dot atop the turquoise. After this has dried, add the small white dot. Add in the purple dot then a smaller yellow dot 'drip' below the navy dots (between the turquoise) and finish the design with a navy dot atop the white centre, allowing the white to just barely peek through.

10 Allow the paint to set overnight, then apply two coats of the protective finish, allowing to dry between coats.

congratulations!

You have made some beautiful-looking rocks of art. What are you going to do with them? Whether you keep them for your own treasures or give them as gifts; put them in a houseplant or brighten up your garden; place them on a shelf or in a little treasure box... the possibilities for decoration and delight are endless. They are sure to bring a colourful piece of happiness wherever they are!

What will you do next? You could take your art to the internet! You will find other artists who love to paint mandala stones, and you could be inspired with new ideas of your own. Take pictures of your stones in various settings, and make a social media page so you can show off your art.

Get inspired and continue your mandala stone journey! If you get stuck, you do not have to look far for ideas. Mandalas are everywhere in nature and life. From a flower in the garden to the shape of a snowflake, inspiration is never more than a stone's throw away.

always remember to think happy dots!

a note on the author

Hi! My name is Katie Cameron and I live in beautiful Halifax, Nova Scotia. I am a postal worker by night and, more recently, mandala-stone maker by day. I have no prior art experience but I have always loved colourful patterns and been fascinated with rocks and minerals. It was in my search of these where I first encountered the works of other great 'dotillists' and knew I had to try making my own mandala stones. It was no time at all before I was hooked on making dots! I created HFXrocks to share these little treasures with the world and have been dotting along ever since.